KU-326-389

FERTILE IMAGE

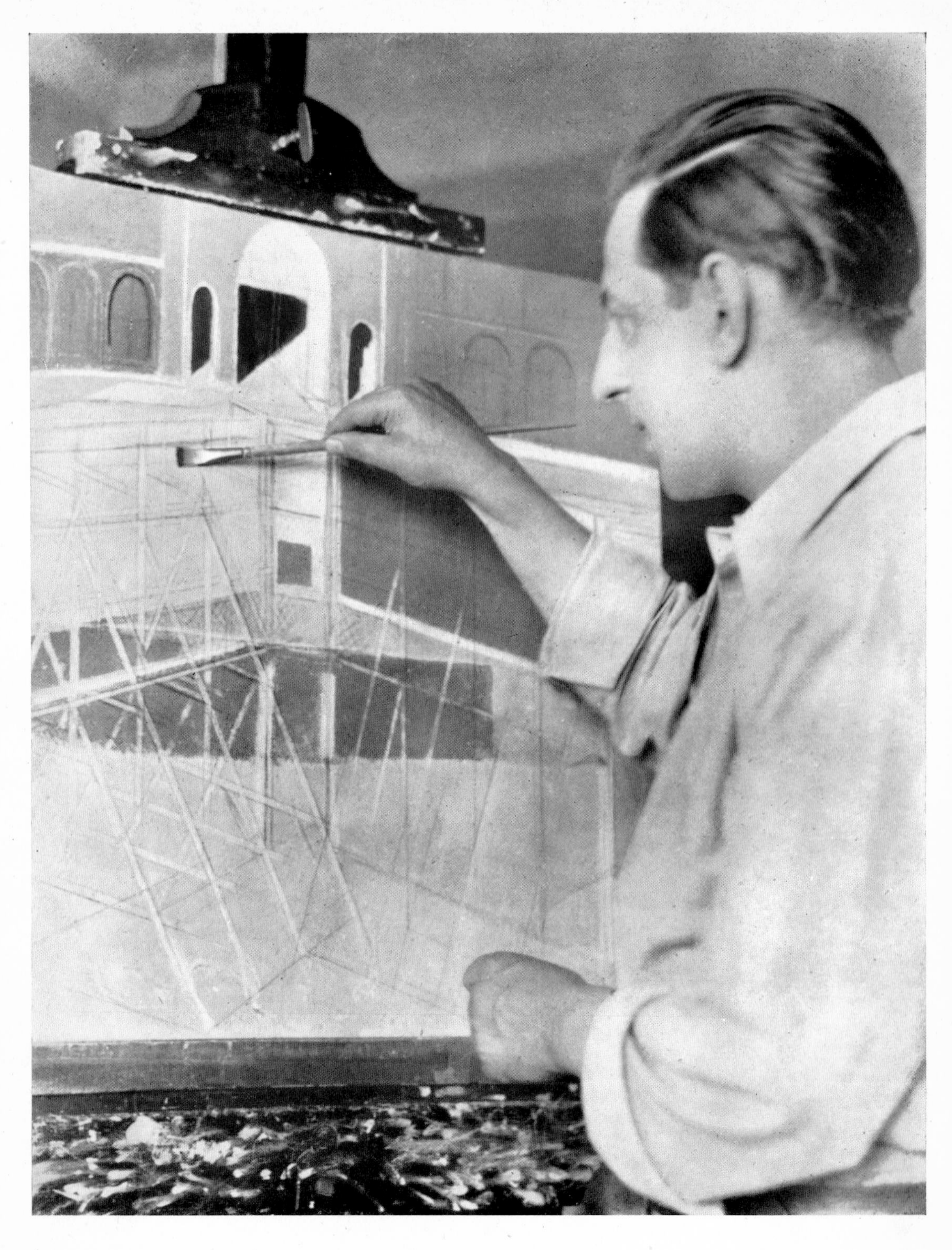

PAUL NASH

(painting the study for 'Northern Adventure', 1929)

FERTILE IMAGE

by PAUL NASH

edited by
MARGARET NASH

with an introduction by
JAMES LAVER

FABER & FABER LIMITED
24 Russell Square
London

First published in mcmli
by Faber and Faber Limited
24 Russell Square London W.C. 1
Printed in Great Britain by
R. MacLehose and Company Limited
The University Press Glasgow

CONTENTS

INTRODUCTION

This is a book of photographs, of photographs taken by an artist, for use in his painting. There is still so much confusion concerning the aims and methods of Art that one can hardly expect such a statement not to be followed by a shrug of the shoulders and the phrase 'Photographs! Oh, well—'. So long as the aim of art is supposed to be some kind of imitation of nature the use of photographs tends to look like cheating. If all you have to do is to copy a photograph the contribution of the painter does not seem very important. One might even ask: Why bother to copy the photograph; why not be content with the photograph itself?

It is true that photographs are sometimes used merely as a crutch. It is not entirely unknown for academic portrait painters to have a photograph of the model taken by a professional photographer. The photograph is then squared up on the canvas with perhaps a slight elongation upwards in order to lend a certain elegance to face and figure. The result is indeed little more than 'a coloured photograph' and one may very well question the legitimacy of the whole process. But photography can be used for quite other purposes.

Walter Sickert was perhaps the last person who could be accused of any academic bias yet he is known in his later years to have used photography extensively; the result, it need hardly be said, was neither photographic nor academic. The Master's signature was written all over it; it was an authentic Sickert. Paul Nash's use of photography, while leading to quite different results, was equally legitimate.

Even from his earliest years there was no question in any of Paul Nash's work of a mere transcription from nature. He was never interested in producing a copy of natural objects. But he was never an abstract painter. Nature, especially landscape, was always his subject matter; he almost invariably used natural objects as a basis for his design.

He began by doing what almost all modern artists do: he either painted direct from actual scenes or he made notes of such scenes and enlarged them to scale in the studio. The former is the method which with the Impressionists became something of a fetish; the second was the method used by nearly all previous painters. Nash used whichever method seemed to him most convenient and most suitable to the work in hand.

Then fell upon him the tragedy of ill health, the delayed result of being gassed while serving as a War Artist during the First World War. As the malady developed it made it increasingly difficult for him to roam about. He therefore developed a method of working from photographs, photographs taken by himself of scenes or objects which arrested his attention. Later, during the Second World War, difficulties of transport and the restriction on photographic material compelled him to dispense with this aid also and he had to a large extent to fall back on his memory and his interior vision. The new situation forced him to change his methods once more. 'I find', he said, 'that, by instinct perhaps, I have adapted my mental process to avoid being defeated by this invincible situation.' Brave words, but then Paul Nash was brave and, up to the final moment, undefeated and undefeatable.

Difficulties and restrictions! It is one of the paradoxes of the creative impulse but such things often work together for good. Coventry Patmore in one of his poems declares that the true poet can find in the restrictions and difficulties of complicated verse forms 'not chains, but wings'. One may well wonder whether the ultimate flowering of Paul Nash's genius would have been reached without all the burdens which his ill health forced upon him. His dream world became ever more real to him, and becomes so to us, until we can walk in it as in a new country of the imagination.

This power of creating a dream world is not shared by every artist. Some of the very greatest have not had it and some lesser artists have possessed it to an astonishing degree. We do not speak of the world of Michelangelo or of Constable; we do speak of the world of Giorgione and of Watteau. Paul Nash had this power and different as his world was from that of Watteau there are perhaps some instructive comparisons to be drawn between them.

Watteau too suffered from ill health but that was not the particular restriction which gave his imagination wings. It so happened that he too had to work at one remove as it were from his subject matter. When he arrived at the studio of his master Gillot he found many canvases showing subjects from the Italian Comedy: Gillot spent most of his time depicting scenes from the actual plays performed. Watteau was inspired to do likewise, but alas! only a few months before, the Italian Comedians had been banished from France for an alleged satire against Madame de Maintenon. What was the result? Instead of portraits of actual actors, instead of pictures of real plays performed, we have the immortal *Gilles* and *L'Embarquement pour Cythère*. A new world of the imagination had been created to which Watteau has left us the key.

That Paul Nash did something comparable will hardly be disputed by anyone who cares for his paintings at all and no consideration of his work can be complete without some attempt to enter this world and to plot, as it were, its essential features. The first thing we notice about it is that it is strangely uninhabited. In all his work whether interior or out of doors there is a singular absence of 'people'. In a letter to Martin Armstrong, who had asked him to illustrate one of his novels, he remarks: 'I don't care for human nature except sublimated or as puppets, monsters, masses formally related to Nature. My anathema is the human "close up". I speak chiefly as an artist—apart from that even I'm not much more tolerant.' He was plainly in reaction against the classical-humanist idea of 'man as the measure of all things'.

Yet when we say that his world was uninhabited and that there were no people in it we must make it clear that we are speaking of humans only. He was himself highly conscious, and he makes us conscious too, of another kind of inhabitation. He felt very strongly the reality of what he calls the object-personage: the standing stone, the gnarled and fallen tree in his eyes and in his hands take on a strange life of their own. Stones in particular seem to have fascinated him.

In a note found among his papers after his death he speaks of his pre-occupation with stones. 'My interest began with the discovery of the Avebury Megoliths when I was staying at Marlborough in the summer of 1933. The great stones were then in their wild state, so to speak. Some were half covered by the grass, others stood up in cornfields or were entangled and overgrown in the copses, some were buried under the turf. But they were wonderful and disquieting, and as I saw them then, I shall always remember them. Very soon afterwards the big work of reinstating the Circles and Avenues began, so that to a great extent that primal magic of the stones' appearance was lost.

'I made some rapid drawings and took several photographs. There was no question of animism here. At that time I had not made the acquaintance of the object-personage. The beauty and mystery of the Megoliths was something peculiar in a different sense, I think mainly a formal sense, their colouring and pattern, Dream.'

Allied to this whole series of pictures concerned with stone objects and object-personages, are some compositions of 'equivalent' objects in relation, set sometimes in open landscape, as in *Equivalents for the Megoliths* and *Objects in Relation*.

During the summer of 1943 he was able to renew his acquaintance with the Avebury Megoliths in the course of a drive while staying at Hungerford. But they were altogether changed in appearance, for the work of reinstating the Circle had been completed. For all his regret at the change Nash still found the effect immensely impressive. He made a few rapid drawings and took a spool of photographs. He wanted to study their disquieting beauty anew. The note ends with a pathetic hope that he might be able to return, to live near them for a time and get to know them again.

It was however not only stones which stimulated his imagination in this way to the point of vision. The painting *Monster Field* in the Durban Art Gallery, Natal, is the final term of a whole series of experiences. Monster Field was for Nash a place of real magic. 'Upon the surface of the green acres which flowed curiously like a wide river over the uplands, there jutted up, as if wading across the tide, two stark objects. They were the remains of two trees, elms, I think, killed by lightning during a furious storm some years ago. So violent had been their overthrow that, utterly, the roots of one had been torn out of the ground. The other had broken off from a splintered shaft upon which it was leaning, its great limbs sprawled backwards over the grass.

'Both trees were by now bleached to a ghastly pallor wherever the bark had broken and fallen away. At a distance in sunlight, they looked literally dead-white, but, at close range, their surfaces disclosed many inequalities of tone and subtle variety of ashen tints. Also, in many places, the bark still clung, a rich, dark plum-coloured brown. Here and there the smooth bole, gouged by the inveterate beetle, let out a trickle of yellow dust which mingled with the red earth of the field.'

Such a passage may serve to show that Paul Nash was no mere dreamer; in him the eye of the pictorial artist was always at work. It also shows that he had powers of literary expression of no mean order. For his imaginative development the discovery of Monster Field was an event of major importance.

'Event' was his own term for such an imaginative experience. There were in his life as an artist a whole series of such events each of which came to him with the shock of revelation and from each of which he went forward, as it were, to the conquest of yet another territory of the mind. Guided by the pictures he has left us we can see these 'events' as guiding the whole of his artistic development. Without them his work would have been quite different. Indeed, it would have been inconceivable.

He records in the admirable fragment of autobiography which he called *Outline* his excitement as a child at discovering that a place could have personality. As yet unaware what he was looking for he found this magic when he was very young in a glade in Kensington Gardens; but it was in a friend's house at Prestwood in Buckinghamshire that the full revelation occurred. From the window of the morning room there was a view of part of the virgin field from which the garden had been made. 'It was undoubtedly', he said, 'the first place which expressed for me something more than its natural features seemed to contain, something which the Ancients spoke of as genius loci—the spirit of a place, but something which did not suggest that the place was haunted or inhabited by a genie in a psychic sense.' He continues 'The place took on a startling beauty, a beauty to my eyes wholly unreal. It was this "unreality", or rather this reality of another aspect of the accepted world, this mystery of clarity which was at once so elusive and so positive, that I now began to pursue and which from that moment drew me into itself and absorbed my life.'

Paul Nash speaks of his life being dominated by a vision, by an emotional experience. With him even more than with most artists it is impossible to distinguish between life and art. Both were inextricably entwined with one another. Indeed the physical disabilities from which he suffered made this inevitable. To him 'events' were milestones in his painting, successive stages in his emotional development. They were, so to say, successive phases of a single dream. For any understanding of his art, therefore, it is necessary to list these 'events' and to try to relate them to the development of his work.

The revelation of childhood has been already dealt with. The next 'event' was concerned with his reactions to the first World War. When hostilities broke out in August 1914 he was in the Lake District on a visit to Gordon Bottomley. Nash enlisted at once as a private in the Artists' Rifles. It is much to be regretted that his autobiography breaks off at this point, but fortunately he left certain notes for its continuance from which it is possible to plot the sequence of events and to gain some notion of his emotional reactions.

He met Rupert Brooke. He was on guard at the Tower of London during the first air raids, but managed to go on painting during the hours of waiting. He was concerned in the early exhibitions of the London Group. He was commissioned in the Hampshires and left for France.

Back in England in hospital after an accident in the trenches he held an exhibition of war drawings, and shortly afterwards he was appointed Official Artist on the Western Front and returned to France. Here he found to his astonishment that he was expected to operate from General Headquarters, but the subjects he wanted to paint were to be found in the front line trenches and after a protracted struggle he succeeded in getting where he wanted to be.

He found the chance he had been waiting for at *Sanctuary Wood at Dawn*; he saw the desolation of Passchendaele. He drew the German front line and the Menin Road; he visited Vimy Ridge. When he returned to England he was able to take with him a considerable body of drawings.

Rather to his surprise they were greeted with enthusiasm by those who had sent him out. He was commanded to hold an exhibition. This took place in May 1918 at the Leicester Galleries, and was an instantaneous success, establishing him at one stroke as a painter of consequence. He made many new friends, including C. R. W. Nevinson, the Sitwells and Arnold Bennett and he was commissioned to paint a large panel for the Imperial War Museum.

There was indeed something quite new in the drawings which the young Nash had brought back from France. There was no burking of the horror and squalor of war. The world he depicted was a dead lunar world, pitted with shell craters, studded with the stems of broken trees which hardly looked as if they had ever been alive, rusted barbed wire creeping all over like some monstrous undergrowth; above, a lowering sky stabbed by searchlights and spotted with flares.

And yet overall was a strange beauty, a highly personal vision and a reality which was nonetheless intense for seeming to exist in a world of dream. But this is not the place to deal with the merits of Nash's war pictures. We are concerned with the war merely as one of the 'events' of his emotional development.

The next 'event' was the discovery of Dymchurch. He became fascinated by the Dymchurch Wall. He made many drawings of its austere banks and platforms with the strange shapes of the waves that beat against its base. He had found a new inspiration in contemporary French painting and, although he was never a cubist, part of the force of the Dymchurch paintings lies in their stylised handling of natural forms. The swell and weight of water is seen almost in mathematical terms, yet even here the artist's personality comes forward so forcibly and his interior vision imposes itself so completely that it is impossible to think of these drawings in terms of influences. Dymchurch becomes merely part of that land of the imagination to which Nash was always adding new territory throughout his life.

It was soon after, at the beginning of 1933, that he began to be ill, really ill from that asthma which he was never afterwards to escape. It was when he was struggling back to life again that he discovered Avebury, and, as we have already related, fell under the spell of the stones.

As, apart from experiences in childhood, the First World War provided the first major 'event' in Paul Nash's life, so the Second World War was to provide the last. Once more he was appointed an Official Artist, this time to the Air Ministry. He began in 1941 a series of commissioned paintings of which the masterpiece is the superb *Totes Meer*: that astonishing vision of wrecked German aeroplanes of which the forms are at once wing tips and the waves of a visionary sea.

By this time his health was getting worse and worse and, as if conscious that the end could not long be delayed, he began the series of Sunflower paintings, symbolising in their strange way his own life, his struggles, his sorrows, his courage and his faith. In the early part of 1946 he developed acute pneumonia and six months later he was dead.

One's first impulse is to be filled with pity for a life so tragically cut short, so frustrated and hampered and so full of suffering. True he had his success but he enjoyed very few of its superficial rewards. He was never a popular painter and throughout his career probably never gained more than a competence from his work. The work itself was his reward and, like Blake, whom he resembles in so many ways, he had no need of riches other than those of his own imagination. To say that he did not live in the real world would be misleading, his world was real enough; he had, so to say, penetrated through the physical appearance of things and come out on the other side.

Most of those who are convinced that they are in touch with reality never even see the objects which lie around them every day; all they see is the labels on the objects. They 'see' a horse, a table or a flower; that is, they make a mental note that such are the names of these things, but they never see the objects themselves and would be quite unable to describe them, even in their most elementary physical aspects. If they did they would be aware that horse, and table, and flower, are full of strangeness, overflowing with personality, charged with *mana*.

Most modern painters have deliberately stopped short of this apprehension. It is true that they *see* the objects, otherwise they could not be painters at all, but they see them merely as related shapes and colours and not as things existing in their own right and with their own significance.

Laurence Binyon once said to Nash, 'You're very Twelfth Century, aren't you?' Nash was surprised but agreed; he knew what Binyon meant, for Binyon was particularly interested in the kind of vision which the twelfth century artist was trying to express.

Modern Western Art has taken a different turn and so perhaps it is easier for us to understand if we change the phrase 'Twelfth Century artist' to Chinese Artist. The Chinese artists of the great Classical schools were hardly at all concerned with the actual appearance of objects. They strove to leave out all that was fortuitous in their outlines and they dispensed with local colour altogether—in this the very opposite of the Pre-Raphaelites who made a fetish of local colour and a religion of particularity. There is a natural affinity between the work of Paul Nash and the ideal landscape of the Oriental Schools.

The other link between them is their shared notion of painting as a kind of ideograph, a sort of calligraphy. French painters of the Modern Schools deal in surfaces and they have always scorned the English for their linear interests. It would be misleading to suggest that all Paul Nash's work was linear, if by that is meant that he was capable of producing nothing but tinted drawings, but the ideograph was always present in his work and that is why every shape in his pictures is charged with a symbolic significance.

We have heard a great deal of symbolic significance within recent years; the drawings of children and lunatics are, we are told, particularly rich in it, and it is the delight of psycho-analysts to chart and explain them. But there is no 'Freudian content' in Nash's work, no obsession with any of the primitive human appetites. Nash was interested in the Surrealists because *they* were interested in the dream, but he was never a Surrealist himself in any formal sense. Still less was he an amateur psychoanalyst. Indeed, to him psycho-analysis 'spoilt it all'. He preferred to have his mysteries unexplained, that is to say he preferred to use mystery as a stimulus to the imagination. There was nothing whatever of the neurotic about Paul Nash; over everything he did he exercised a calm control. He was a contemplative, almost a mystic, and his sole passion was the cultivation of the interior life.

We have contrasted him with the Pre-Raphaelites who are sometimes thought of as the most typical English painters but the real English tradition is quite different, for there *is* an English tradition in spite of the fanatics who until recently could see nothing good in English painting which was not imported from France. French painting has its own value and a high one, but the attempt to import it into England has always been a mistake. Within the last twenty years the English tradition has produced a body of work which owes little or nothing to foreign influences and which is in complete reaction against the aesthetic theories current in the early 'twenties.

The newly discovered interest in Samuel Palmer has been partly responsible: Palmer with his systematic brooding over the poetical content of landscape until he was able to distil its essence into his work. Paul Nash owed nothing to Palmer directly; he had already discovered his manner for himself but he was part of the general movement which led to a frank acceptance of the poetic quality of English landscape. This does not in the least mean that he was an illustrator in the bad sense of the word. It could never be said of him that 'Every picture tells a story'. The content of his work is always 'poetic' only in the sense that it expresses an emotional theme, an imaginative attitude. It would be impossible to express it in words, just as it is impossible to express in prose what a poem is 'about'. What it is about is the poem itself.

England is not a land of clear edges; its landscape is blue-veiled and mysterious even in sunlight, and this quality is always in Paul Nash's paintings. But they are saved from fading away in mere indefiniteness by the bold structure of their calligraphic line which even when it is not immediately obvious is always present. He never ceased to be a draughtsman striving for the realised form.

It is time to return to the photographs, which are remarkable enough merely as photographs, quite apart from their importance for the understanding of Paul Nash's painting. Using an ordinary camera without gadgets of any kind and without pretending in any way to a professional technique, he learned to 'paint with light' to some purpose. There is nothing 'arty' about his photographs: they are clear and definite, and absolutely untouched, yet his instinctive feeling for design made every one of his plates something of a work of art.

In the first photograph, of *Old Harry Rock*, there is something obviously beautiful, in the sense that anybody looking for the picturesque might have taken it, admiring the strange rock-form less for its own sake than for its situation, the dramatic light on its face, the blurred vista of infinite sea behind. In the second photograph, we see the real artist at work, for the ordinary eye would never even have noticed these low groins or have thought there was any purpose in photographing them. Yet here they are: a design of astonishing simplicity and force. Indeed, so forceful is their pattern that they grow in scale as one looks at the photograph until they become, not a little wooden barrier that we might step over, but a vast mediæval castle with towers and curtain walls.

What made the sea-shore so peculiarly fascinating to Nash was his sense of form and movement, his feeling for the complementary and interlocking rhythms of land and sea. The weight of stones, the weight of water, perpetual movement, intense repose: these were the themes which kept recurring in his mind, so that he was able to play with them, as it were, and even to transpose them. A painting like *Stone Sea*, in the collection of Mrs. Malcolm L. McBride, shows what he was thinking. Waves have, when you come to think of it, the structural solidity of stone walls, and stone walls have a surge and rhythm, as they curve over the landscape, comparable to the waves of the sea.

As we turn over the photographs of the Dorset group, we seem to see him picking his way over the stones, graduating, one might almost say, from an interest in the heap to an interest in the individual, to the discovery, as he might have phrased it, of the 'object-personage'. Such an object-personage is the strangely impressive *Gate Post* (Plate 20) with its clean-cut lines and lichened face, and from this it is but a step to the monoliths which always so potently affected his imagination. Plainly, he loved them all whether in the rough but vigorously logical forms of Nature's hewing, or shaped with the man-made purpose of Stonehenge. The first that he actually labels *Stone Personage* is a little of both, Nature and man collaborating to produce this brooding Avebury sentinel.

Then, suddenly, he seems to realise that a tree is a kind of monolith also, and we are given the marvellous photograph of *Dead Tree, Romney Marsh*, with its proud upward thrust and the infinite subtlety of its curves. But if a tree is like a standing stone its rough bark twists and turns like the waves of the sea. And we realise that the artist has imparted to us his way of looking at things, the freshness and unity of his vision.

The importance of the *Monster Field* photographs has been already stressed. *Stalking Horse* and *Laocoon* tell their own story; and suddenly the artist's eye is caught by something quite different, something one would hardly have expected him to be interested in at all. In most of his objects he found a delight which was due at least in part to their revelation of the logic of chance. Thus the wave broke, thus the tree fell, and one can see that it could not have been otherwise. Earth and heaven have worked together to produce this twisted shape. But in topiary everything is small and fiddling and man-made, and we would not have expected the trimmed tree and the clipped hedge to find a place in Nash's dream world. Yet *The Haunted Garden* undoubtedly does so. It is nearer to the precipice edge of the pretty than is at all common in his work, but it retains its magic and the personal quality of his vision. Yet, so far as the present writer is aware, it was never used as the basis of a painting.

One has to say the same, alas, of many of the photographs that follow! Surely the exciting, unexpected view of *The Bull Ring, Ronda*, should have been the starting point for a whole new series of pictorial discoveries. The *Dye Pits of Tetuan* are something new again, and so are his experiments in photo-montage and double-exposure. With the final photographs we are on firmer ground, for several of them were used, some of them directly, as in *Totems*, and the *Atlantic* series, some as starting points of form or rhythm. But all, used or unused, whether we see their purpose or not, are signed with Paul Nash's hand. They are all highly personal and meaningful, so that even in these photographs we can feel our imagination heightened, and be made citizens of the dream world of which he made us free.

NOTES ON THE PHOTOGRAPHS

1. Old Harry Rock, Ballard Head, Dorset

The Old Harry group of rocks are at the point of boundary where the Dorset and Hampshire shores meet. Amongst the Dorset people these well-known rocks are named 'Old Harry and his Wife'. It is 'Old Harry' who is pictured here as the 'wife' has lost her height and is no longer so impressive.

2. The Shore, Dymchurch, Kent

This view of the wooden breakwaters which intersect the whole of the Dymchurch shore is one of Paul Nash's earliest experiments with documentary photography. It was taken about 1931 and was used as a record for various pictures of the Dymchurch shore carried out about this time. Notice the contrast not only between the forms but also between the textures: the smooth sand and the lace-edge of the incoming wave. The artist's eye for a pattern is well shown in the converging lines and balanced light and shade.

3. Seashore, Dorset

This and the eight following photographs show parts of the Dorset coast from Purbeck Isle to the great bituminous rock of Kimmeridge Bay. The view of waves from a height reveals the artist's preoccupation with the natural pattern-making of incoming waves. He has seized 'the moment of expressive movement', no easy thing in a photograph. Failure to do so results in the curious frozen effect of many snapshots.

4. The Shore, Kimmeridge Bay, Dorset

The formation of the rocks, standing like a wall against the sea, is a feature of this sea-coast, the cliff being made up here of alternative soft shale and hard shaley stone, in regular bands. To quote from *The Dorset Guide* written by Paul Nash: 'This is the first straight view of the Purbeck coast, a low wall of black cliffs, steely blue at some angles of the sun's light when they appear crusted with emerald green moss. The shores beneath present the wildest chaos. Stones and boulders of all kinds, sizes and forms seem to have been hurled and scattered over the smooth, gleaming platform of the shale. Fantastic seaweeds, wreckage and the flashing pools bewilder the sight. . . . From now on the coast is an iron wall seeming to be literally built of huge great black blocks.'

5. Rock Formation, Kimmeridge Bay

It is as if Nature had laid down a crazy pavement but with bigger and more impressive blocks and with a logic of her own. The dappled effect is due to the different angles of the stone surfaces towards the light; and the greater number of light surfaces towards the left gives something of the effect of an oncoming wave. In Paul Nash's imagination the forms of different objects were constantly related and inter-changed.

6. Sea Coast, Dorset

Almost a 'professional' photograph with its blend of the very near and the very far, the massive, patterned rocks of the foreground sharp against the misty distance of the receding coast; but there is more than this in the artist's pleasure and interest. Whether consciously or not, he relates the texture of the ground at his feet to that of the sea, and the distant land to the nearby rocks, so that the houses, seen from far away, become, as it were, a kind of lichen, echoing and carrying on the surface pattern near his eye.

7. Breakwater

A scene in Dorset but suggesting the mood of the Dymchurch drawings and paintings. A composition of hard, horizontal lines with the subtle diagonal of the irregular wooden groin leading the eye to the softer horizontal of the sea. There is an austerity here of the kind which appealed strongly to Paul Nash, as if everything were more logical and simplified than it usually is in Nature. It is as if he said: 'Let us see what Nature—and I—can do with the utmost economy of means.'

8. The Flats, Sea Coast, Dorset

The flat 'pavement' broken up by the action of the sea. It is almost as if the scattered stones were themselves waves hurling themselves against a causeway. Aristotle defined genius as 'the power of perceiving analogies'. In Paul Nash's reactions to natural scenes there was often a kind of visual punning, although the word has fallen into such disrepute that one hesitates to use it. It is now recognized, however, that the unconscious deals almost entirely in puns: that is in accidental resemblances endowed with a new significance. Perhaps 'design' is nothing other than the exploitation of this fact.

9. Stones and Seaweed, Study 1

Once more unexpected resemblances—'correspondences' as the occultists would call them—offer a stimulus to the artist's imagination. Here the vegetation becomes the sea, spilling over the rounded rocks with something of the effect of a waterfall. As the fronds of sea-weed have actually been placed in position by the water, they are, so to speak, the markers of the receding wave, the visible ghosts of the vanished sea.

10. Stones and Seaweed, Study 2

The interest in this photograph is centred upon the seaweed itself with the flattened arch of its stem, its strange root and its drooping fronds. There is something monstrous about it as there is about so many aquatic plants, something almost animal. We grow so much accustomed to the tidily hidden roots of land plants that there is something almost shocking in the naked, clinging tentacles, as of an octopus waiting for its prey.

11. The Shore, Portland Bay

There are certain crystalline rock formations so regular that it is hard to believe that they have never been chipped and shaped by the hand of man. This is a piece of Nature's quarrying, linked by implication with the photograph that follows.

12. The Quarry, Portland Bill

Man's quarrying, for contrast. The great stones lie upon one another like the blocks in a child's box of bricks. They build up to a kind of pyramid and the point from which the photograph has been taken, with the deep hollow on the right, has, one feels, been chosen to emphasise this effect. But the picture is also a study in surface texture, particularly with regard to the tool marks in light and shade.

13. The Cliffs, Portland Bay

This, and the preceding photograph, portray the formidable region of solid limestone which contains the noted prison and is approached by the Chesil bank. The following quotation from *The Dorset Guide* describes these dramatic features of the coast: 'Immense rocks of square shape have been loosened and dislodged by the powerful sea, and piled up above the foot of the cliffs. Here the Portland Race sets in, a current so strong that it is felt as far away as Aldhelm's Head. . . . Behind the cliffs, with their cloven rock, their massive platforms, the derricks are seen to stride across the sky. The earth yawns and gives up gigantic white blocks. We think of London on a bright day, when the black soot contrasts so happily with the white Portland stone.'

14. Old Quarry Hut, Swanage

This, and the three following photographs, were taken as a record of a particular kind of arrangement of the stone in the building of walls in the Purbeck Isle district. Nash had the artist's appreciation of any unmechanical craft, and the building of a wall without mortar has nothing mechanical about it. The stones must be selected and grouped with a care which takes account of their irregular shapes and sizes if the wall is to hold. The process imposes a pattern, and has its own reward.

15. Rock Wall, Dorset

A curious effect of upward surge in the way the stones are placed. One hardly knows whether a wall of this nature is the work of human hands or not. It might equally well be a fragment of some 'Giant's Causeway' or the legendary walls of Thebes.

16. Stone Wall, Worth Matravers, Study 1

The stones are arranged in a manner which has been traditional from Roman times. This method of placing stones on top of one another gives a rhythmic movement to the wall which Paul Nash afterwards used in a water-colour called *Stone Sea.*

17. Stone Wall, Worth Matravers, Study 2

The ordered arrangement of the *Stone Sea* broken like a wave approaching the land, the crest rising white and menacing as it is about to fall. Paul Nash had an acute perception of the fundamental structure even of so evanescent a thing as a breaking wave. He felt its weight and inevitability, and here he seems to insist on one of those similarity-contrasts which are so often implicit in his work.

18. Stone Wall Opening, Study 1

Unless the climbing ivy gave us the scale, the wall in its monumental solidity might be the bastion of some ancient city. Paul Nash's imagination was continually playing with these effects of scale, sometimes deliberately dwarfing the 'Old Harry Rock' until it looks like a boundary post, sometimes lending a low groin the effect of a mediæval castle; he was constantly reminding us that the artist, like Alice in Wonderland, has the gift of making himself larger and smaller at will, so that at one moment, although 'bounded in a nutshell', he is the king of infinite space, and at another can see all eternity in a grain of sand.

19. Stone Wall Opening, Study 2

Another view of the same opening in the wall, with attention focused on the surface texture of the tree across which the shadow falls, the pattern of light on dark, the pattern of dark on light. Equally rich in suggestion is the contrast between the dark edge of one wall and the dazzling white of the other, the white rounded lichens and the dark spiky ivy contrasting both in tone and shape.

20. Stone Gate Post

Already referred to in the Introduction, p. 18. The surface texture of the stone must have been an added attraction. The more closely one looks at this stone gate-post the more beautiful it becomes.

21. Monolith in Arcadia

This, and the four following photographs of the monoliths, were used as models for a series of pictures both in water-colour and oils, painted during the four years previous to the war. They were all taken either at Avebury or Stonehenge.

22. Avebury Sentinel

This splendid photograph, as well as No. 24, was used in the water-colour entitled *Landscape of the Megalith*, painted in 1937, and also in the oil painting *Circle of the Monolith.*

23. Stonehenge, Study 1

By comparison with those at Avebury, the Stonehenge monoliths seem almost too smooth and sophisticated. These massive stones have lost the sense of being natural objects and the awe they inspire is of a different kind: a wonder at the power of man to transport such monuments hither and to make them, as it were, form a circle round him and dance to his tune.

24. Stone Personage, Avebury

Used, with No. 22, as model and inspiration for *Landscape of the Megalith* and *Circle of the Monolith.* The stone is indeed charged with *mana*, and is, as the artist called it, a 'personage' in its own right.

25. Stonehenge, Study 2

Once more, the contrast with Avebury is emphasised. The monolith in the foreground is not so much a 'personage' as a functionary, a hierophant engaged, with others, in the ordered performance of a rite. What are these standing stones, indeed, but the fossilized gestures of those who once formed a circle on the sward and turned in unison to salute the sun?

26. Palm Tree Trunk, Nice

In the arrangement of the scales of the palm tree Paul Nash saw an echo of the Dorset walls and of his imagined *Stone Sea.* That so powerful an upward thrust should be expressed by horizontal lines, that the stones of the base, as it were, should be so interlocked to support the lighter, more regular, tiers above, and that the whole should be alive, these were the things which impelled the artist to pause before a palm tree that the ordinary passer-by would hardly have noticed.

27. Dracula

Strangely twisted roots had a particular fascination for the artist. Here the 'poised object' seems to be climbing up the wall with sinister intent, like Dracula climbing up to the window of the castle in Bram Stoker's famous story. But, in addition to this, there is the oft-recurring motif of the wave, or rather of a series of waves, advancing shoreward and breaking into white edges as they waver and fall back.

28. Dead Tree, Romney Marsh

There is hardly a detail of this natural object which does not accord with one of the artist's preoccupations.

29. Tree Wound

A study in the contrasting textures of bark and wood. The tree has been blasted, like Semele, by the love of Zeus, and from such a wound might the youthful Dionysus have sprung to life. Yet Paul Nash's mythology was never formulated in terms of a personal Olympus. His gods are still imprisoned in the half-hewn stone and his dryads are more tree than woman.

30. Tree Trunk, Study 1

A study of bark, the flaws and twists of which produce natural patterns in (if the phrase may be permitted) waves of wood.

31. Tree Trunk, Study 2

Another study of bark, the beautiful regularity of the structure on the left side of the tree contrasting with the no less beautiful whorls and knots of the right.

32. Monster Field, Study 1

33. Monster Field, Study 2

For a commentary on these photographs and how they were related to pictures, see Introduction, p. 4. See also *Monster Field*, by Paul Nash (Counterpoint Publications, Oxford, 1946):

'We are not studying two fallen trees that look like animals, but two monster objects outside the plan of natural phenomena. What reference they have to life should not be considered in relation to their past—therein they are dead—they now excite our interest on another plane, they have "passed on" as people say. These now inanimate natural objects are alive in quite another world; but, instead of being invisible like so many of that huge community, or only made visible by the complicated machinery of spiritualism, they are so much with us that I was able to photograph them in full sunlight. . . . Both as a painter and as a collector of objects, it was impossible for me to ignore the occupants of Monster Field.'

34. Stalking Horse

Directly employed for a water-colour bearing the same title, now unfortunately destroyed by fire. The tree has been torn up by the roots and the accidental shape of these suddenly came alive in the artist's imagination, so much alive that one is tempted to discard the obvious meaning of the title. Here the horse is himself the hunter, alert and watchful, tracking down his prey.

35. Laocoon

Directly employed for a water-colour bearing the same title, and very closely resembling the photograph from which it was drawn. Full of the menace which Paul Nash so often found in natural objects, it is more frightening than the famous marble group from which it takes it name. Here the snakes have amalgamated into one creature, kraken or octopus, which has already overcome and engulfed its victims.

36. Waterfall, Study 1

This beautiful design can be looked at from any angle: it retains its suggestive power. It might be anything: water, or smoke: hair blown by the wind or ghost 'from an enchanter fleeing'. Once more, only the ivy gives us the scale.

37. Waterfall, Study 2

When we look at a photograph like this, it is as if we had never seen the beauty of falling water before: the contrasting darkness of its transparent shadows, the whiteness of its spray.

38. Waterfall, Study 3

The most mysterious of the four studies, and perhaps the most evocative. The permanent in the impermanent; the 'passing away of passing away'.

39. Waterfall, Study 4

The end of the fall when the water once more becomes stream instead of 'water-smoke', finds its level and 'comes down to earth again'.

40. Meadow Grass and Stones

The 'wave' of grass, with an artist's interest in the textures of the gravel surfaces, rough and smooth.

41. Portrait of Mrs. Simpkins (Carnation Border)

Paul Nash rarely photographed vegetation, particularly garden vegetation, for its own sake. Here again he is concerned with contrasting textures, with the breaking wave movement of the grass and with the star-like pyrotechnics of the carnation plants.

42. The Haunted Garden

The photograph referred to in the Introduction, p. 18.

43. The Grotto at 3 Eldon Grove, N.W. 3

This grotto was made at the bottom of the garden at the Nashs' house in Hampstead, with the help of an Italian workman, who in true traditional manner cemented the oyster shells on to the rough sandstone with which he had built the grotto. It has been used in the oil painting at the Tate, entitled *Grotto in the Snow*, and it has also been painted as a water-colour of that name which is now in a Canadian private collection.

44. The Bull Ring, Ronda, Spain

The crudely stencilled numbers on the wooden seats of the bull ring make, in perspective, an entrancing pattern. The eye of the artist for the exact spot from which to take his picture was never used with better effect.

45. Moorish Quarter, Tetuan, North Africa

It is impossible to say which excited the artist more, the contrasting textures or the pattern of light and shade. It was these that interested him rather than the undeniable picturesqueness of the whole scene.

46. The Defenders of Maiden Castle

These photographs were taken at Maiden Castle near Dorchester, during the excavations which were being carried out on that site by Dr. Mortimer Wheeler in 1934 or 1935. The skeletons are of those who fell in battle against the Roman invaders.

47. Nest of Skeletons

The skeletons of two Ancient Britons: warriors in the first flush of manhood, to judge by the preservation of the teeth.

48. Dye Pits, Tetuan, North Africa, Study 1

Taken during a visit to North Africa in 1934. The photograph shows the dye pits used for dyeing the Arab shoes, one of the trades of Tetuan. So regular and inevitable seems the form of the vats that it is as if some gigantic mollusc had left his abandoned shell upon the shore.

49. Cactus

Taken during Paul Nash's visit to Tetuan. He was fascinated by the purely formal qualities of these monstrous plants which seem to combine the personality of the animal with the stillness of the standing stone.

50. Dye Pits, Tetuan, North Africa, Study 2

Another study of dye pits, their irregular lines contrasting with the more stylised shapes in No. 48. Oddly enough, these, rather than the others, are more plainly the work of man.

51. Empty Room. Photo Montage

An example of photo-montage. This and the following photographs (Nos. 52 to 60) are all parts of photographic experiments made in connection with a passing interest in Surrealism. The effect is at once strangely convincing and oddly sinister, as if the broken pavement and shattered room had been encountered in a dream.

52. Step Edge

An experiment in sunlight and shade. Shown at the Surrealist Exhibition at the New Burlington Galleries in 1937. Here there is no imposing of one pattern on another by the artist: the shadow of the bough does all that is required to set the imagination working.

53. Spanish Dream

An experiment in double exposure. One of the most interesting of the 'Surrealist' photographs.

54. Stone Roundels

The patterns revealed by sunlight on the surface of old mill stones, beautifully grooved to facilitate the escape of the ground grain.

55. Flowering Stones

A study in light and shade, the curious pattern emphasised by the shadow of the operator and the sharp brim of his hat.

56. Ditch

Shown at the Surrealist Exhibition at the New Burlington Galleries in 1937. There is a deliberate attempt to surprise the eye by an unexpected angle of vision, and to tease the mind with unfamiliar aspects of familiar things. The drainage pipe which looks like the stalk of a plant, the white fronds that seem to hang over the edge of an abyss, the dog's footprints (is it a dog?) in the cement: all have the effect of making us question accepted images. The deep cleft down the middle of the picture is accepted as a symbol of the unconscious process of dissociation.

57. Fleur du Mal

Another cactus study. This plant had for Paul Nash a significance as of something threatening and evil. It seemed to him like some monstrous, many-headed animal, about to strike.

58. Root Study

A gnarled root clinging to the wall like some gigantic squid. A recurring motif in Paul Nash's photographs. Compare *Dracula* (No. 27) and *Laocoon* (No. 35).

59. Marsh Personage

Shown at the Surrealist Exhibition at the New Burlington Galleries in 1937. One of the 'objects' which the artist loved to collect as a stimulus to his imagination. He thought so highly of this one that he took it home and set it up in his studio, the curved portion attached to the larger piece like a billowing sail.

60. Objet Trouvé

Another of the 'objects', even more full of 'personality' than the last: a kind of infant monster looking upon the strange world of our normality with intense curiosity, and for the first time.

61. Study of Wood Fencing

The regular lines of wooden palings could be as exciting to the artist as the gnarled trunks of old trees, especially when, as here, the sunlight adds its pattern. It is as if the eye glides over the palings like the fingers over the strings of a harp.

62. Totems, Old Shipyard, Rye

The photograph shows the wooden posts formerly used in the shipbuilding trade of Rye Harbour. They seem indeed to be totems of a vanished race. This particular photograph was directly used in a water-colour with the same title, now the property of the Graves Art Gallery, Sheffield.

63. Atlantic Voyage, Study 1

These two photographs were part of a set taken during the voyage home from America in 1931. They were very useful records for a series of water-colours, of which *Atlantic* is well-known.

64. Atlantic Voyage, Study 2

The clean lines of the boat derrick, the taut ropes, the logical purpose are in violent contrast to some of the twisted shapes seen before. Here we have left the haunted garden; we have come out of the wood; the 'personages' no longer confront us. Here problems of stress and balance are resolved, and the whole composition imparts a curious sense of peace.

PLATES

EDITOR'S NOTE

All the photographs included in this book were taken by my husband, Paul Nash, between the years 1931-1946, with the aid of a No. 2 Kodak Camera which I gave him when we visited the United States in 1931.

1. OLD HARRY ROCK, BALLARD HEAD, DORSET

THE SHORE, DYMCHURCH, KENT

3. SEASHORE, DORSET

4 THE SHORE, KIMMERIDGE BAY, DORSET

5. ROCK FORMATION, KIMMERIDGE BAY

6. SEA COAST, DORSET

7. BREAKWATER

8. THE FLATS, SEA COAST, DORSET

9. STONES AND SEAWEED, STUDY 1

10. STONES AND SEAWEED, STUDY 2

11. THE SHORE, PORTLAND BAY

12. THE QUARRY, PORTLAND BILL

13. THE CLIFFS, PORTLAND BAY

14. OLD QUARRY HUT, SWANAGE

15. ROCK WALL, DORSET

16. STONE WALL, WORTH MATRAVERS, STUDY 1

17. STONE WALL, WORTH MATRAVERS, STUDY 2

18. STONE WALL OPENING, STUDY 1

19. STONE WALL OPENING, STUDY 2

20. STONE GATE POST

21. MONOLITH IN ARCADIA

22. AVEBURY SENTINEL

23. STONEHENGE, STUDY I

24. STONE PERSONAGE, AVEBURY

25. STONEHENGE, STUDY 2

26. PALM TREE TRUNK, NICE

27. DRACULA

28. DEAD TREE, ROMNEY MARSH

29. TREE WOUND

30. TREE TRUNK, STUDY I

31. TREE TRUNK, STUDY 2

32. MONSTER FIELD, STUDY I

33. MONSTER FIELD, STUDY 2

34. STALKING HORSE

35. LAOCOON

36. WATERFALL, STUDY I

37. WATERFALL, STUDY 2

38. WATERFALL, STUDY 3

39. WATERFALL, STUDY 4

40. MEADOW GRASS AND STONES

41. PORTRAIT OF MRS. SIMPKINS

42. THE HAUNTED GARDEN

43. THE GROTTO AT 3 ELDON GROVE, N.W. 3

44. THE BULL RING, RONDA, SPAIN

45. MOORISH QUARTER, TETUAN, NORTH AFRICA

46. THE DEFENDERS OF MAIDEN CASTLE, DORSET

47. NEST OF THE SKELETONS

48. DYE PITS, TETUAN, NORTH AFRICA, STUDY I

49. CACTUS

50. DYE PITS, TETUAN, NORTH AFRICA, STUDY 2

51. EMPTY ROOM. PHOTO MONTAGE

52. STEP EDGE

53. SPANISH DREAM

54. STONE ROUNDELS

55. FLOWERING STONES

56. DITCH

57. FLEUR DU MAL

58. ROOT STUDY

59. MARSH PERSONAGE

60. OBJET TROUVÉ

61. STUDY OF WOOD FENCING

62. TOTEMS, OLD SHIPYARD, RYE

63. ATLANTIC VOYAGE, STUDY 1

64. ATLANTIC VOYAGE, STUDY 2